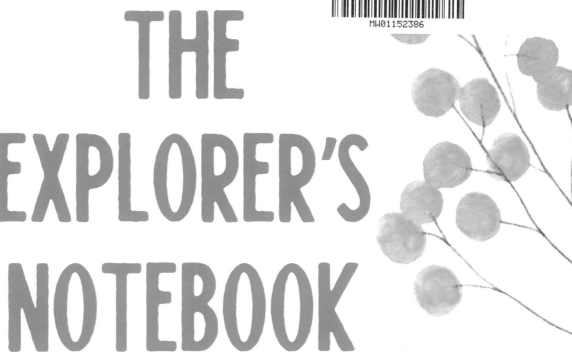

THE EXPLORER'S NOTEBOOK

Field Trips, Travels, and Explorations of the Curious Mind

THE WORLD IS WAITING FOR YOU

BY: TINA WANN

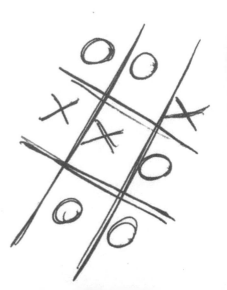

To Chris, Elijah, and Rylee.
You all make me a better human.

INTRODUCTION

Welcome to The Explorer's Notebook! This is a place for you to record all of your explorations, vacations, and travels. Life is about creating moments and collecting memories. Whether you are exploring the patch of woods next to your home or a new city, you have a place to record all of your findings.

SPECIAL NOTE FOR HOMESCHOOL FAMILIES

There is a box on the first journal page called "Hours in the Field." This is meant to be used by homeschool families who need to track hours. After each field trip, make sure your child records how much time was spent learning.

HOW TO USE THESE PAGES

Each place you explore has four pages dedicated to recording your findings.
Journal Page One lets you rate your trip, write down pro tips, and so much more.
Journal Page Two has spaces to draw photos of your favorite parts and mark it on the map.

The next two pages are my favorite. These pages provide big open spaces for you to tape or glue in brochures, leaves, and other treasures you collect. Check out **#theexplorersnotebook** on Instagram to see how others are using these pages.

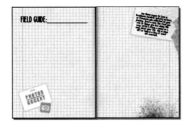

If four pages is more than you need for each place you explore, divide it up and record your findings in a way that works for you. There are several other pages to record things too. I'm not going to give any more instruction, because after all, this is your notebook.

Make sure to take photos of your completed pages and upload them to Instagram with **#theexplorersnotebook** so others can see all of your amazing work.

YOUR MISSION:

I, _____, AM AN EXPLORER. MY MISSION IS TO DOCUMENT AND OBSERVE THE WORLD AROUND ME. I WILL TAKE NOTES, COLLECT THINGS, COPY, TRACE, AND LEARN. I WILL DOCUMENT MY TRAVELS, RECORD WHAT I AM DRAWN TO, AND FOCUS ON ONE THING AT A TIME.

TIPS FOR USING THIS NOTEBOOK:

1. BE FEARLESS. TAPE, GLUE, SPLATTER, AND COLLECT. MAKE THIS BOOK YOUR OWN. EVERY BLANK SPACE IS YOUR CANVAS TO CAPTURE MEMORIES.

2. CARRY THIS BOOK AND A GREAT PEN WITH YOU IF YOU CAN!

3. CHECK OUT #THEEXPLORERSNOTEBOOK ON INSTAGRAM TO SEE WHAT OTHER EXPLORERS ARE DOING.

4. IF YOU DON'T KNOW WHAT TO DO, MAKE IT UP. CREATE YOUR OWN RULES FOR THIS JOURNAL.

THE EXPLORER'S NOTEBOOK
TABLE OF CONTENTS

EACH TIME YOU TAKE AN ADVENTURE,
ADD THE PAGE AND DESTINATION HERE
SO YOU CAN FIND IT LATER.

Page

Destination

Hey Explorer,
Color in each state
you have visited!

STATES I'VE VISITED

8

COLOR A FLAG FOR EACH COUNTRY YOU HAVE VISITED

GO...

- [ ] on a picnic
- [ ] fishing
- [ ] kayaking
- [ ] geocaching
- [ ] on a bike ride
- [ ] for a night swim
- [ ] hiking
- [ ] ziplining
- [ ] to the pool
- [ ] snorkeling
- [ ] cliff jumping
- [ ] to the drive in theater
- [ ] to a live show
- [ ] to a sporting event
- [ ] star gazing
- [ ] on a tour
- [ ]
- [ ]
- [ ]

VISIT...

- [ ] an art museum
- [ ] a science museum
- [ ] a history museum
- [ ] a children's museum
- [ ] a Little Free Library
- [ ] an amusement park
- [ ] a cave
- [ ] an annual festival
- [ ] an aquarium
- [ ] a waterfall
- [ ] a farmer's market
- [ ] the beach
- [ ] an arcade
- [ ] a zoo
- [ ] a national park
- [ ] a landmark
- [ ]

TRAVEL CHALLENGES

- [ ] build a sand castle
- [ ] jump in the ocean or lake
- [ ] try a new food
- [ ] sit by a campfire
- [ ] catch fireflies
- [ ] walk barefoot outside
- [ ] find a hag stone
- [ ] make a smashed penny
- [ ] watch the sunset
- [ ] watch the sunrise
- [ ] take a class
- [ ] ride go carts
- [ ] play mini golf
- [ ] ride a horse
- [ ] eat at a food truck
- [ ] learn a new skill
- [ ] watch a concert
- [ ] see a play
- [ ] pick berries

Activities to Try

- [ ] _____
- [ ] _____
- [ ] _____
- [ ] _____
- [ ] _____
- [ ] _____
- [ ] _____
- [ ] _____
- [ ] _____
- [ ] _____
- [ ] _____
- [ ] _____
- [ ] _____
- [ ] _____
- [ ] _____

Places to Travel

- [ ] _____
- [ ] _____
- [ ] _____
- [ ] _____
- [ ] _____
- [ ] _____
- [ ] _____
- [ ] _____
- [ ] _____
- [ ] _____
- [ ] _____
- [ ] _____
- [ ] _____
- [ ] _____
- [ ] _____

TRAVEL GOALS!

DESTINATION: _____

HOURS IN THE FIELD: _____

DATE: _____

ON A SCALE OF 1 - 10

| 1 | 2 | 3 | 4 | 5 | 6 | 7 | 8 | 9 | 10 |

CORRESPONDENCE

POSTCARD

FOR ADDRESS ONLY

U.S. POSTAGE ONE CENT

LET'S DO THIS AGAIN!

TRAVEL NOTES!

EXPLORER TIPS:

① _____

② _____

③ _____

3 THINGS I LEARNED

12

Find it on the map

I DIDN'T LIKE...

I WANT TO KNOW

BEST PART

BOOKS I READ

Author

Title

Book #

Due Date | Borrower's Name

FOOD I ATE

13

FIELD GUIDE:_____

PHOTOS ARE A RETURN TICKET TO A MOMENT

14

Use these pages to tape in brochures, receipts, tickets, pictures, or treasures you collected on your journey. Draw a map, the food you ate, or things you saw along the way. Write a story, a poem, or a song about your trip. Rub in some dirt or tape in a bag of sand! Get creative.

DESTINATION: _____

HOURS IN THE FIELD: _____

DATE: _____

ON A SCALE OF 1 - 10

1 2 3 4 5 6 7 8 9 10

CORRESPONDENCE

POSTCARD

FOR ADDRESS ONLY

U.S. POSTAGE ONE CENT

LET'S DO THIS AGAIN!

TRAVEL NOTES!

EXPLORER TIPS:

1 _____

2 _____

3 _____

3 THINGS I LEARNED

16

Find it on the map

I DIDN'T LIKE...

I WANT TO KNOW

BEST PART

BOOKS I READ

Author		
Title		Book #
Due Date	Borrower's Name	

FOOD I ATE

FIELD GUIDE: _____

PHOTOS
ARE A RETURN TICKET TO A
MOMENT

Use these pages to tape in brochures, receipts, tickets, pictures, or treasures you collected on your journey. Draw a map, the food you ate, or things you saw along the way. Write a story, a poem, or a song about your trip. Rub in some dirt or tape in a bag of sand! Get creative.

19

DESTINATION: _____   DATE:_____
HOURS IN THE FIELD: _____   ON A SCALE OF 1 - 10
1 2 3 4 5 6 7 8 9 10

CORRESPONDENCE

POSTCARD
FOR ADDRESS ONLY

U.S. POSTAGE
ONE CENT

LET'S DO THIS AGAIN!

TRAVEL NOTES!

EXPLORER TIPS:

1 _____
2 _____
3 _____

3 THINGS I LEARNED

20

Find it on the map

I DIDN'T LIKE...

I WANT TO KNOW

BEST PART

BOOKS I READ

Author		
Title		Book #
Due Date	Borrower's Name	

FOOD I ATE

21

FIELD GUIDE: _____

PHOTOS ARE A RETURN TICKET TO A MOMENT

22

Use these pages to tape in brochures, receipts, tickets, pictures, or treasures you collected on your journey. Draw a map, the food you ate, or things you saw along the way. Write a story, a poem, or a song about your trip. Rub in some dirt or tape in a bag of sand! Get creative.

DESTINATION: _____

HOURS IN THE FIELD: _____

DATE: _____

ON A SCALE OF 1 - 10

1 2 3 4 5 6 7 8 9 10

CORRESPONDENCE

POSTCARD
FOR ADDRESS ONLY

U.S. POSTAGE
ONE CENT

LET'S DO THIS AGAIN!

TRAVEL NOTES!

EXPLORER TIPS:

1 _____

2 _____

3 _____

3 THINGS I LEARNED

24

Find it on the map

I DIDN'T LIKE...

I WANT TO KNOW

BEST PART

BOOKS I READ

Author			
Title			Book #
Due Date	Borrower's Name		

FOOD I ATE

25

FIELD GUIDE: _____

PHOTOS
ARE A RETURN TICKET TO A
MOMENT

Use these pages to tape in brochures, receipts, tickets, pictures, or treasures you collected on your journey. Draw a map, the food you ate, or things you saw along the way. Write a story, a poem, or a song about your trip. Rub in some dirt or tape in a bag of sand! Get creative.

DESTINATION: _____

HOURS IN THE FIELD: _____

DATE: _____

ON A SCALE OF 1 - 10

1 2 3 4 5 6 7 8 9 10

CORRESPONDENCE

POST CARD

FOR ADDRESS ONLY

U.S. POSTAGE
ONE CENT

LET'S DO THIS AGAIN!

TRAVEL NOTES!

EXPLORER TIPS:

1 _____

2 _____

3 _____

3 THINGS I LEARNED

28

Find it on the map

I DIDN'T LIKE...

I WANT TO KNOW

BEST PART

BOOKS I READ

Author		
Title		Book #
Due Date	Borrower's Name	

FOOD I ATE

29

FIELD GUIDE: _____

PHOTOS
ARE A RETURN TICKET TO A
MOMENT

Use these pages to tape in brochures, receipts, tickets, pictures, or treasures you collected on your journey. Draw a map, the food you ate, or things you saw along the way. Write a story, a poem, or a song about your trip. Rub in some dirt or tape in a bag of sand! Get creative.

DESTINATION: _____   DATE: _____

HOURS IN THE FIELD: _____   ON A SCALE OF 1 – 10

1 2 3 4 5 6 7 8 9 10

CORRESPONDENCE

POSTCARD

FOR ADDRESS ONLY

U.S. POSTAGE ONE CENT

LET'S DO THIS AGAIN!

TRAVEL NOTES!

EXPLORER TIPS:

1 _____

2 _____

3 _____

3 THINGS I LEARNED

32

Find it on the map

I DIDN'T LIKE...

I WANT TO KNOW

BEST PART

BOOKS I READ

Author

Title   Book #

Due Date   Borrower's Name

FOOD I ATE

33

FIELD GUIDE:_____

PHOTOS
ARE A RETURN TICKET TO A
MOMENT

34

Use these pages to tape in brochures, receipts, tickets, pictures, or treasures you collected on your journey. Draw a map, the food you ate, or things you saw along the way. Write a story, a poem, or a song about your trip. Rub in some dirt or tape in a bag of sand! Get creative.

DESTINATION: _____

HOURS IN THE FIELD: _____

DATE: _____

ON A SCALE OF 1 - 10

| 1 | 2 | 3 | 4 | 5 | 6 | 7 | 8 | 9 | 10 |

CORRESPONDENCE

POSTCARD

FOR ADDRESS ONLY

U.S. POSTAGE
ONE CENT

Long!

Madras

LET'S DO THIS AGAIN!

TRAVEL NOTES!

EXPLORER TIPS:

1 _____
2 _____
3 _____

3 THINGS I LEARNED

36

Find it on the map

I DIDN'T LIKE...

I WANT TO KNOW

BEST PART

BOOKS I READ

Author

Title | | Book #

Due Date | Borrower's Name |

FOOD I ATE

37

FIELD GUIDE:_____

PHOTOS
ARE A RETURN TICKET TO A
MOMENT

38

Use these pages to tape in brochures, receipts, tickets, pictures, or treasures you collected on your journey. Draw a map, the food you ate, or things you saw along the way. Write a story, a poem, or a song about your trip. Rub in some dirt or tape in a bag of sand! Get creative.

DESTINATION: _____

HOURS IN THE FIELD: _____

DATE: _____

ON A SCALE OF 1 - 10

1 2 3 4 5 6 7 8 9 10

CORRESPONDENCE

POSTCARD
FOR ADDRESS ONLY

U.S. POSTAGE ONE CENT

LET'S DO THIS AGAIN!

TRAVEL NOTES!

EXPLORER TIPS:

① _____
② _____
③ _____

3 THINGS I LEARNED

40

Find it on the map

I DIDN'T LIKE...

I WANT TO KNOW

BEST PART

BOOKS I READ

Author		
Title		Book #
Due Date	Borrower's Name	

FOOD I ATE

FIELD GUIDE:_____

PHOTOS
ARE A RETURN TICKET TO A
MOMENT

42

Use these pages to tape in brochures, receipts, tickets, pictures, or treasures you collected on your journey. Draw a map, the food you ate, or things you saw along the way. Write a story, a poem, or a song about your trip. Rub in some dirt or tape in a bag of sand! Get creative.

DESTINATION: _____   DATE: _____

HOURS IN THE FIELD: _____   ON A SCALE OF 1 - 10
 1 2 3 4 5 6 7 8 9 10

CORRESPONDENCE

POSTCARD
FOR ADDRESS ONLY

U.S. POSTAGE
ONE CENT

LET'S DO THIS AGAIN!

TRAVEL NOTES!

EXPLORER TIPS:

1 _____
2 _____
3 _____

3 THINGS I LEARNED

44

Find it on the map

I DIDN'T LIKE...

I WANT TO KNOW

BEST PART

BOOKS I READ

Author

Title   Book

Due Date   Borrower's Name

FOOD I ATE

45

FIELD GUIDE: _____

PHOTOS
ARE A RETURN TICKET TO A
MOMENT

46

Use these pages to tape in brochures, receipts, tickets, pictures, or treasures you collected on your journey. Draw a map, the food you ate, or things you saw along the way. Write a story, a poem, or a song about your trip. Rub in some dirt or tape in a bag of sand! Get creative.

DESTINATION: _____

HOURS IN THE FIELD: _____

DATE: _____

ON A SCALE OF 1 - 10

| 1 | 2 | 3 | 4 | 5 | 6 | 7 | 8 | 9 | 10 |

CORRESPONDENCE

POSTCARD

FOR ADDRESS ONLY

U.S. POSTAGE
ONE CENT

LET'S DO THIS AGAIN!

TRAVEL NOTES!

EXPLORER TIPS:

1 _____

2 _____

3 _____

3 THINGS I LEARNED

48

Find it on the map

I DIDN'T LIKE...

I WANT TO KNOW

BEST PART

BOOKS I READ

Author

Title   Book #

Due Date   Borrower's Name

FOOD I ATE

49

FIELD GUIDE:_____

PHOTOS ARE A RETURN TICKET TO A MOMENT

Use these pages to tape in brochures, receipts, tickets, pictures, or treasures you collected on your journey. Draw a map, the food you ate, or things you saw along the way. Write a story, a poem, or a song about your trip. Rub in some dirt or tape in a bag of sand! Get creative.

DESTINATION: _____ DATE: _____

HOURS IN THE FIELD: _____ ON A SCALE OF 1 - 10

1 2 3 4 5 6 7 8 9 10

CORRESPONDENCE

POSTCARD

FOR ADDRESS ONLY

U.S. POSTAGE
ONE CENT

LET'S DO THIS AGAIN!

TRAVEL NOTES!

EXPLORER TIPS:

① _____
② _____
③ _____

3 THINGS I LEARNED

52

Find it on the map

I DIDN'T LIKE...

I WANT TO KNOW

BEST PART

BOOKS I READ

Author

Title   Book #

Due Date   Borrower's Name

FOOD I ATE

FIELD GUIDE: _____

PHOTOS ARE A RETURN TICKET TO A MOMENT

Use these pages to tape in brochures, receipts, tickets, pictures, or treasures you collected on your journey. Draw a map, the food you ate, or things you saw along the way. Write a story, a poem, or a song about your trip. Rub in some dirt or tape in a bag of sand! Get creative.

DESTINATION: _____

HOURS IN THE FIELD: _____

DATE: _____

ON A SCALE OF 1 - 10

1 2 3 4 5 6 7 8 9 10

CORRESPONDENCE

POSTCARD

FOR ADDRESS ONLY

U.S. POSTAGE ONE CENT

LET'S DO THIS AGAIN!

TRAVEL NOTES!

EXPLORER TIPS:

1 _____

2 _____

3 _____

3 THINGS I LEARNED

56

Find it on the map

I DIDN'T LIKE...

I WANT TO KNOW

BEST PART

BOOKS I READ

Author		
Title		Book #
Due Date	Borrower's Name	

FOOD I ATE

57

FIELD GUIDE:_____

PHOTOS ARE A RETURN TICKET TO A MOMENT

Use these pages to tape in brochures, receipts, tickets, pictures, or treasures you collected on your journey. Draw a map, the food you ate, or things you saw along the way. Write a story, a poem, or a song about your trip. Rub in some dirt or tape in a bag of sand! Get creative.

DESTINATION: _____

HOURS IN THE FIELD: _____

DATE: _____

ON A SCALE OF 1 – 10

[1] [2] [3] [4] [5] [6] [7] [8] [9] [10]

CORRESPONDENCE

POSTCARD

FOR ADDRESS ONLY

U.S. POSTAGE ONE CENT

LET'S DO THIS AGAIN!

TRAVEL NOTES!

EXPLORER TIPS:

1 _____
2 _____
3 _____

3 THINGS I LEARNED

Find it on the map

I DIDN'T LIKE...

I WANT TO KNOW

BEST PART

BOOKS I READ

Author

Title

Book

Due Date   Borrower's Name

FOOD I ATE

FIELD GUIDE:_____

PHOTOS
ARE A RETURN TICKET TO A
MOMENT

62

Use these pages to tape in brochures, receipts, tickets, pictures, or treasures you collected on your journey. Draw a map, the food you ate, or things you saw along the way. Write a story, a poem, or a song about your trip. Rub in some dirt or tape in a bag of sand! Get creative.

DESTINATION: _____

HOURS IN THE FIELD: _____

DATE: _____

ON A SCALE OF 1 - 10

1 2 3 4 5 6 7 8 9 10

CORRESPONDENCE

POSTCARD

FOR ADDRESS ONLY

U.S. POSTAGE ONE CENT

LET'S DO THIS AGAIN!

TRAVEL NOTES!

EXPLORER TIPS:

1 _____

2 _____

3 _____

3 THINGS I LEARNED

64

Find it on the map

I DIDN'T LIKE...

I WANT TO KNOW

BEST PART

BOOKS I READ

Author		
Title		Book #
Due Date	Borrower's Name	

FOOD I ATE

FIELD GUIDE: _____

PHOTOS ARE A RETURN TICKET TO A MOMENT

Use these pages to tape in brochures, receipts, tickets, pictures, or treasures you collected on your journey. Draw a map, the food you ate, or things you saw along the way. Write a story, a poem, or a song about your trip. Rub in some dirt or tape in a bag of sand! Get creative.

DESTINATION: _____

HOURS IN THE FIELD: _____

DATE: _____

ON A SCALE OF 1 - 10

1 2 3 4 5 6 7 8 9 10

CORRESPONDENCE

POSTCARD
FOR ADDRESS ONLY

U.S. POSTAGE
ONE CENT

LET'S DO THIS AGAIN!

TRAVEL NOTES!

EXPLORER TIPS:

① _____

② _____

③ _____

3 THINGS I LEARNED

Find it on the map

I DIDN'T LIKE...

I WANT TO KNOW

BEST PART

BOOKS I READ

Author		
Title		Book #
Due Date	Borrower's Name	

FOOD I ATE

69

FIELD GUIDE:_____

PHOTOS
ARE A RETURN TICKET TO A
MOMENT

70

Use these pages to tape in brochures, receipts, tickets, pictures, or treasures you collected on your journey. Draw a map, the food you ate, or things you saw along the way. Write a story, a poem, or a song about your trip. Rub in some dirt or tape in a bag of sand! Get creative.

DESTINATION: _____

HOURS IN THE FIELD: _____

DATE:_____

ON A SCALE OF 1 - 10

1 2 3 4 5 6 7 8 9 10

CORRESPONDENCE

POSTCARD
FOR ADDRESS ONLY

U.S. POSTAGE
ONE CENT

LET'S DO THIS AGAIN!

TRAVEL NOTES!

EXPLORER TIPS:

1 _____
2 _____
3 _____

3 THINGS I LEARNED

Find it on the map

I DIDN'T LIKE...

I WANT TO KNOW

BEST PART

BOOKS I READ

Author		
Title		Book #
Due Date	Borrower's Name	

FOOD I ATE

FIELD GUIDE: _____

PHOTOS
ARE A RETURN TICKET TO A
MOMENT

74

Use these pages to tape in brochures, receipts, tickets, pictures, or treasures you collected on your journey. Draw a map, the food you ate, or things you saw along the way. Write a story, a poem, or a song about your trip. Rub in some dirt or tape in a bag of sand! Get creative.

DESTINATION: _____

HOURS IN THE FIELD: _____

DATE: _____

ON A SCALE OF 1 - 10

1 2 3 4 5 6 7 8 9 10

CORRESPONDENCE

POSTCARD

FOR ADDRESS ONLY

U.S. POSTAGE ONE CENT

Long.

Meridian of

Madras

LET'S DO THIS AGAIN!

TRAVEL NOTES!

EXPLORER TIPS:

1 _____

2 _____

3 _____

3 THINGS I LEARNED

Find it on the map

I DIDN'T LIKE...

I WANT TO KNOW

BEST PART

BOOKS I READ

Author

Title   Book #

Due Date   Borrower's Name

FOOD I ATE

FIELD GUIDE:_____

PHOTOS ARE A RETURN TICKET TO A MOMENT

Use these pages to tape in brochures, receipts, tickets, pictures, or treasures you collected on your journey. Draw a map, the food you ate, or things you saw along the way. Write a story, a poem, or a song about your trip. Rub in some dirt or tape in a bag of sand! Get creative.

DESTINATION: _____

HOURS IN THE FIELD: _____

DATE: _____

ON A SCALE OF 1 - 10

1 2 3 4 5 6 7 8 9 10

CORRESPONDENCE

POSTCARD

FOR ADDRESS ONLY

U.S. POSTAGE
ONE CENT

LET'S DO THIS AGAIN!

TRAVEL NOTES!

EXPLORER TIPS:

1 _____

2 _____

3 _____

3 THINGS I LEARNED

80

Find it on the map

I DIDN'T LIKE...

I WANT TO KNOW

BEST PART

BOOKS I READ

Author

Title

Book #

Due Date | Borrower's Name

FOOD I ATE

FIELD GUIDE:_____

PHOTOS
ARE A RETURN TICKET TO A
MOMENT

82

Use these pages to tape in brochures, receipts, tickets, pictures, or treasures you collected on your journey. Draw a map, the food you ate, or things you saw along the way. Write a story, a poem, or a song about your trip. Rub in some dirt or tape in a bag of sand! Get creative.

DESTINATION: _____

HOURS IN THE FIELD: _____

DATE: _____

ON A SCALE OF 1 - 10

| 1 | 2 | 3 | 4 | 5 | 6 | 7 | 8 | 9 | 10 |

CORRESPONDENCE

POST CARD

FOR ADDRESS ONLY

U.S. POSTAGE ONE CENT

Longt°

Meridian of G

Madras

LET'S DO THIS AGAIN!

TRAVEL NOTES!

EXPLORER TIPS:

1. _____

2. _____

3. _____

3 THINGS I LEARNED

DERIK VIII. LAND NORTH EAST FORELAND

GREENLAND

Find it on the map

I DIDN'T LIKE...

I WANT TO KNOW

BEST PART

BOOKS I READ

Author

Title

Book #

Due Date | Borrower's Name

FOOD I ATE

85

FIELD GUIDE:_____

PHOTOS ARE A RETURN TICKET TO A MOMENT

86

Use these pages to tape in brochures, receipts, tickets, pictures, or treasures you collected on your journey. Draw a map, the food you ate, or things you saw along the way. Write a story, a poem, or a song about your trip. Rub in some dirt or tape in a bag of sand! Get creative.

DESTINATION: _____

HOURS IN THE FIELD: _____

DATE: _____

ON A SCALE OF 1 - 10

| 1 | 2 | 3 | 4 | 5 | 6 | 7 | 8 | 9 | 10 |

CORRESPONDENCE

POSTCARD

FOR ADDRESS ONLY

U.S. POSTAGE ONE CENT

Longt

Meridian of G

Madras

LET'S DO THIS AGAIN!

TRAVEL NOTES!

EXPLORER TIPS:

1 _____

2 _____

3 _____

3 THINGS I LEARNED

Find it on the map

I DIDN'T LIKE...

I WANT TO KNOW

BEST PART

BOOKS I READ

Author		
Title		Book #
Due Date	Borrower's Name	

FOOD I ATE

FIELD GUIDE: _____

PHOTOS
ARE A RETURN TICKET TO A
MOMENT

90

Use these pages to tape in brochures, receipts, tickets, pictures, or treasures you collected on your journey. Draw a map, the food you ate, or things you saw along the way. Write a story, a poem, or a song about your trip. Rub in some dirt or tape in a bag of sand! Get creative.

WRITING PROMPTS

1. Write a letter to a friend recommending a place to visit.

2. People watch. Make up stories about the people around you.

3. Writing the details for a trip that you wish you could take.

4. Write a list of adjectives that describe your last trip.

5. You get to move into one place you visited. Where do pick and why?

6. Use your 5 senses to describe your current location.

7. Write about an interesting person you met on a trip.

8. Pick a home in the town you are visiting. Make up a story about the people who live there.

9. Pretend you are waking up at midnight to go on an outing. Write about what you experience.

10. Write about something you learned on a trip.

11. Free write!

This Journal Belongs to:

_____

107

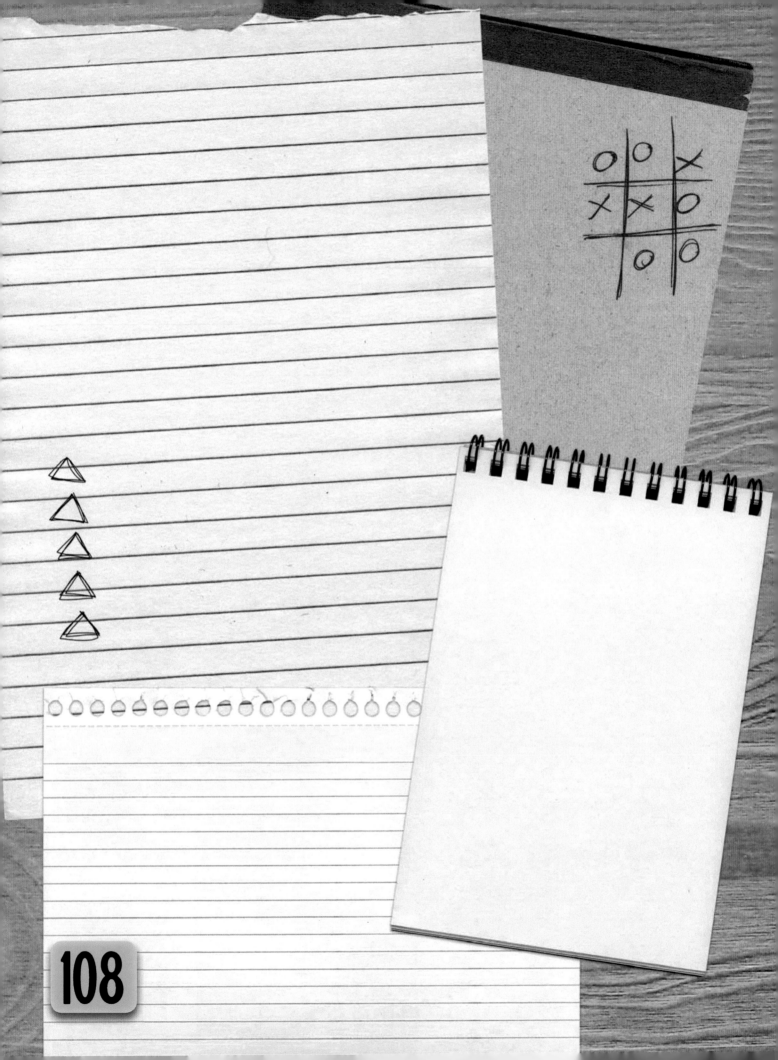

110

MOST PEACEFUL
PLACE

Best City

AWARD
WINNING
MOMENTS

Biggest Surprise

Best Performance

Tallest Attraction

Best View

112

MOST EXCITING
EXPERIENCE

FUNNIEST
MOMENT

Best Outdoor
Adventure

Coolest Thing to See

Coolest Animal
We Saw

WOW!!!

Most Beautiful Place

Best Indoor
Adventure

113

EXPLORE MORE

Most Surprising!

Life Changing Moment

MOST THRILLING

Best Museum

Best Zoo

MOST JAW DROPPING

Best Food

114

CREATE YOUR
OWN AWARDS

115

Made in the USA
Middletown, DE
15 December 2020